TOXIC CREATURES

The Puffer Fish

Alicia Z. Klepeis

Cavendish Square

New York

Published in 2018 by Cavendish Square Publishing, LLC
243 5th Avenue, Suite 136, New York, NY 10016

Library of Congress Cataloging-in-Publication Data

Names: Klepeis, Alicia, 1971- author.
Title: The puffer fish / Alicia Z. Klepeis.
Description: New York : Cavendish Square Publishing, [2018] | Series: Toxic creatures | Includes index.
Identifiers: LCCN 2016052781 (print) | LCCN 2016058115 (ebook) | ISBN 9781502625953 (paperback) |
ISBN 9781502625823 (6 pack) | ISBN 9781502625908 (library bound) | ISBN 9781502625830 (E-book)
Subjects: LCSH: Puffers (Fish)--Juvenile literature.
Classification: LCC QL638.T32 K54 2018 (print) | LCC QL638.T32 (ebook) | DDC 597/.64--dc23
LC record available at https://lccn.loc.gov/2016052781

Editorial Director: David McNamara
Editor: Fletcher Doyle
Copy Editor: Nathan Heidelberger
Associate Art Director: Amy Greenan
Designer: Alan Sliwinski
Production Coordinator: Karol Szymczuk
Photo Research: J8 Media

Printed in the United States of America

CONTENTS

A colorful puffer fish looks harmless but may be deadly.

CHAPTER ONE

A Puffer Fish Primer

Puffer fish are unusual animals. Sometimes they have lean bodies and round, bulging heads. Other times they look like living beach balls. These fish may appear harmless, but look out! Many puffer fish are deadly.

Puffers are water creatures. Most live in **tropical** and subtropical ocean waters. They are found around the world in the Atlantic, Pacific, and Indian Oceans. Puffer fish have almost never been seen in cold water.

An adult dwarf puffer fish swims inside an aquarium. These fish are native to India.

About 29 species of puffers live in freshwater. Others survive in **brackish** water. There are more than 120 species in all.

Not all puffer fish look alike. Some are tiny. The dwarf, or pygmy, puffer can be less than 1 inch (2.5 centimeters) long! Others are big. The giant puffer can be more than 2 feet (61 cm) long. Some puffer fish are brightly colored. This coloring may warn **predators** to stay away!

Other puffers have less bright coloring. They may blend in with their environment. This can help them avoid being hunted.

Not Easy Prey

Puffers are rather slow and clumsy swimmers. However, they have an amazing defense strategy. When threatened, they will take in large amounts of water (and sometimes air). This quickly swells their

The colors of this is bright puffer fish may scare off predators on a coral reef near Komodo, Indonesia.

bodies to two or three times their normal size. Some puffers also have very rough skin, or spikes that stick out of their skin when inflated. These defenses make it hard for an enemy to eat the puffer fish.

Not all puffer fish live by the same schedule. Some, like the dog-faced puffer, are active during the day. Others, such as the white-spotted puffer, are active at night.

An inflated puffer fish swims in its ocean habitat. Its spiky skin helps protect it from predators.

A young star puffer fish hovers along the sea floor in the tropical waters of Indonesia's Lembeh Strait.

Puffers don't normally make a surprise attack on **prey** from a hidden location. Instead, they usually feed on slow-moving or stationary animals. Puffer fish look for food by probing the sea floor. They also check the nooks and crannies found in coral. Puffers have big, sensitive lips. These allow them to tell prey apart from objects such as rocks.

Puffers have four teeth that form a beak-like structure. It can crush the shells of oysters and clams. This wears down their razor-sharp teeth, which grow throughout their lives. These teeth have taken off the fingertips of fishermen who were removing the puffers from the hook.

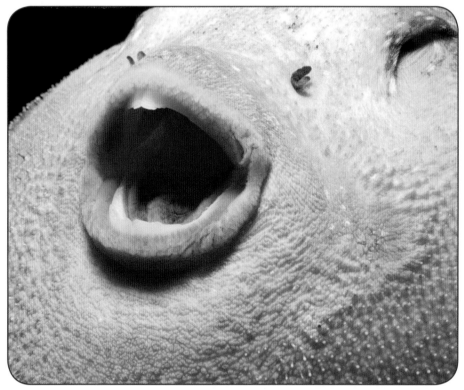

This inflated guineafowl puffer shows its sharp teeth. These puffers are found in the Pacific Ocean.

They Eat Everything

What do puffers eat? They are omnivores, which means they eat plants and animals. Their diet includes fish, **algae**, worms, sponges, and more.

The life-span of puffer fish is typically four to eight years. Puffer fish are oviparous, meaning they lay eggs. Each female will lay three to seven eggs. The hard shell of the eggs protects baby puffer fish until they hatch. Once they hatch, the young swim immediately.

Puffer larvae are not immediately as poisonous as their parents. They have not built up their stores of poison yet. Luckily, puffer moms give some poison to their young. Scientists have found this poison in the eggs and on the surface of puffer fish larvae. It might not be enough to kill a predator. Some predators that try to eat puffer fish larvae spit them out.

Puffer Fish Quick Facts

Scientific name: *Tetraodontidae* (Latin for "four teeth").

Common name: Puffer fish (and sometimes blowfish); in Japan, prepared puffer fish is called fugu. This comes from the Chinese characters for "river" and "pig."

Range: Most commonly found in tropical and subtropical waters of Indian, Pacific, and Atlantic Oceans; also found in some freshwater and brackish waters.

Size: Vary widely in size, from less than 1 inch (2.5 cm) to about 3 feet (0.9 meters) long

How many kinds: There are more than 120 species of puffer fish.

Fun Fact: It's illegal to serve puffer fish to the emperor of Japan as one puffer fish has enough poison to kill thirty adult humans.

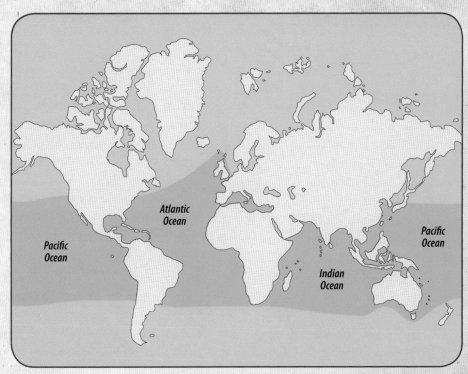

The puffer fish lives in the areas marked in green, which are the warmer regions of the world's oceans.

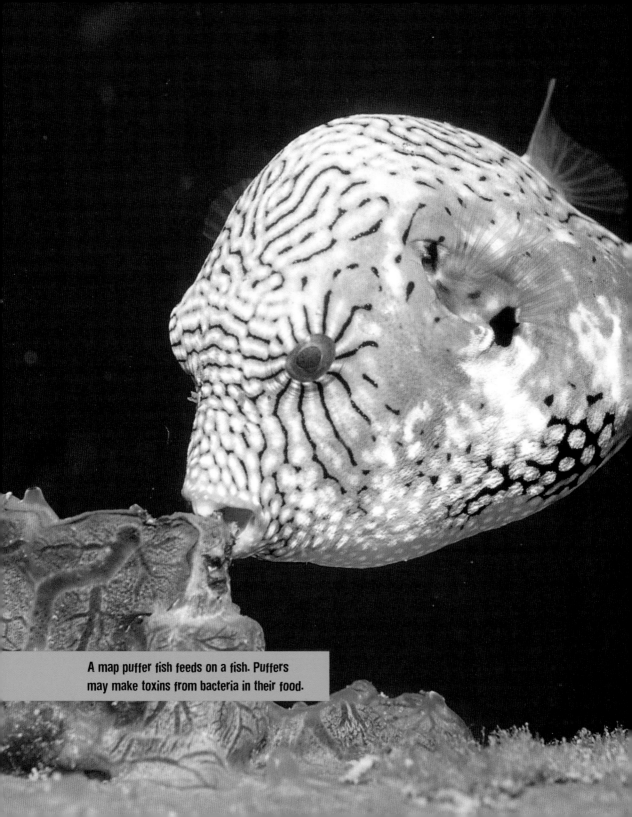

A map puffer fish feeds on a fish. Puffers
may make toxins from bacteria in their food.

Puffer Fish Poison

Most people are frightened by puffer fish. This makes sense given how poisonous some of them are. Poisonous animals make **toxins** that are harmful when touched or eaten. Puffer fish are poisonous. This is different from being venomous. Venomous creatures inject venom into their prey. They can use fangs, spines, or stingers to do this. The puffer's spikes do not inject any venom.

The poison that puffers use is called tetrodotoxin. Where does it come from? Unlike some creatures, puffer fish do not make their own toxin. Scientists think puffers get this toxin from the food chain. Bacteria produce tetrodotoxin. These bacteria are eaten by creatures that are then eaten by other animals that are eaten by puffer fish. Puffers become toxic by gathering and storing the toxin in their tissues. The toxic species of puffers can withstand about five hundred to one thousand times more tetrodotoxin in their bodies than nontoxic puffer fish or other fish.

Diet Affects Toxin

You might be surprised to learn that toxic puffer fish can be made nontoxic. How? By changing their diet. When toxic puffers are raised in aquariums with bacteria-free, filtered water, they become nontoxic.

Chefs in Tokyo carefully separate the parts of the puffer fish as they prepare fugu.

For many puffer species, the liver and **ovaries** are the most toxic, followed by their intestines and skin. But for some freshwater and brackish-water puffers, their skin is the most poisonous.

How do people and animals get poisoned by puffer fish? By eating them. When toxic puffers encounter enemies, they excrete tetrodotoxin from their skin. This makes them taste terrible, so

A reef lizardfish, one of the few animals immune to the poison of a puffer, eats a puffer fish in the Coral Sea.

predators often spit them out—fast! But the unlucky ones who eat poisonous puffers can die.

Deadly for Humans

Puffers are the world's second most poisonous **vertebrates**. (The golden poison dart frog is first.) Each poisonous puffer contains enough toxin to kill thirty adult humans. Tetrodotoxin is 1,200 times more poisonous than cyanide. A lethal dose for people is tiny than the head of a pin. It takes just 10 *billionths* of a gram to kill a mouse.

Are there any animals that can safely eat puffer fish? Yes. Tiger sharks and sea snakes are immune to their poison. So are lizardfish.

When a person eats puffer fish, the effects can be terrifying. Even if the fish is prepared properly, diners might experience numbness in their lips and tongue. These sensations often disappear. But sometimes the fish has not been prepared right. The person who ate the fish might develop a headache or nausea. He or she might throw up. In more extreme cases, the victim will lose the ability to move parts of his or her body. The toxin gradually shuts down the central nervous system. It **paralyzes** nerves and muscles. This will cause the victim to have trouble breathing and can lead to death. The effects of the poison can start acting in minutes, and death usually happens within hours.

Deaths from eating puffer fish in Japan have fallen since the 1980s. Each year, zero to six people die, but other people get poisoned while eating . For the victims who don't die, the experience is horrible. Tetrodotoxin does not make a person unconscious. Victims are alert and awake the whole time the poison is in their system.

No Antidote

There is no known **antidote** to tetrodotoxin. If a victim is brought to the hospital on time, doctors will often pump out his or her stomach.

Victims also may be put on a machine to keep them breathing. It's no wonder that puffers often appear on the top-ten list of the most toxic animals on Earth!

Captain Cook's Unusual Discovery

People disagree about where and when it was discovered that puffer fish were toxic. Written records discussing puffer fish from China and Egypt are thousands of years old. In September 1774, explorer Captain James Cook recorded in his log the effects of puffer fish poison. Members of his crew had numbness and shortness of breath after eating the fish. Some pigs on board ate the remains of the puffers and died.

Captain James Cook explored the Pacific Ocean.

Puffer fish are safe as long as their habitat stays healthy.

Learning from Puffer Fish

P uffer fish are toxic creatures. They are not endangered. Most populations of puffers are stable, but some species are vulnerable. Pollution and overfishing threaten their populations. Habitat loss is another problem for some puffers. For example, *Tetraodon pustulatus* is only found in the Cross River in Nigeria and Cameroon. Scientists worry that oil exploration could threaten the existence of

Green spotted puffers can survive in both freshwater and marine environments.

this species. So could other environmental damage in Korup National Park, where this puffer lives.

Puffer fish can poison both people and animals. Still, people around the globe eat them. Seems strange, right? In Japan, puffer meat is considered a delicacy. It's known as fugu. People pay hundreds of dollars for a serving. Puffer poison does not disappear after cooking. Most Japanese chefs serve fugu raw and sliced thinly.

Hard to Prepare

Chefs in Japan who want to serve fugu must train hard. They study for years to learn how to prepare

A plate of thinly sliced fugu (or puffer fish) sashimi awaits a brave eater.

A master fugu chef removes the skin as he prepares a puffer fish in a restaurant in Tokyo, Japan.

it properly. They have to remove all the poisonous
parts from the fish. Why? Otherwise the diner might

die! Fugu chefs-in-training have to take a written exam. Then they have to prepare the puffer fish— and eat it!

Many trainees fail the test.

Besides being an exotic food source, puffer fish have other value to people. Puffer poison may help people. How? By using it to treat chronic pain. Many cancer patients go through chemotherapy. Morphine is often used as a painkiller for this treatment. Researchers have come up with a painkiller based on tetrodotoxin. It is three thousand times stronger than morphine. Also, the puffer poison medicine does not have the side effects of nausea or addiction. Researchers are now trying this new pain reliever with a small group of cancer patients. Hopefully, puffer fish toxin can be used to help more people in the future.

Toxic Creatures Quiz

1. How do puffer fish defend themselves?

2. Are all puffer fish toxic?

3. What does puffer fish toxin do to victims?

4. What benefits do puffers have for the world?

Answer Key

1. When threatened, they will take in large amounts of water (and sometimes air). They swell their bodies up fast. The spikes on some puffers stick out when inflated. It's hard to eat the puffer fish in this state.

2. No. Many species are poisonous, but some are harmless. The toxic puffers can become nontoxic if put into water without tetrodotoxin-producing bacteria.

3. It affects their central nervous system. The poison paralyzes nerves and muscles. It can make people unable to breathe and sometimes leads to death.

4. Some people around the world enjoy eating their meat. Scientists can make pain-killing medicine from their poison to help cancer patients.

GLOSSARY

algae A plant or plantlike organism (like seaweed) that includes forms mainly growing in water.

antidote A remedy that fixes the effects of a poison.

brackish Slightly salty, such as when river water and seawater are mixed.

ovary A female reproductive organ where eggs are produced.

paralyze To make an animal unable to move, act, or function.

predator An animal that lives by killing and eating other animals.

prey An animal that is hunted or killed by another animal for food.

toxin A substance produced by a living organism (such as a bacterium) that is very poisonous to other organisms.

tropical A region that never gets frost and that has temperatures warm enough for plants to grow all year long.

vertebrate An animal that has a backbone or spinal column.

FIND OUT MORE

Books

Leigh, Autumn. *Deadly Pufferfish*. Small but Deadly. New York: Gareth Stevens Publishing, 2011.

Pettiford, Rebecca. *Puffer Fish*. Ocean Life Up Close. Minnetonka, MN: Bellwether Media, 2017.

Websites

National Geographic Kids: Pufferfish

http://kids.nationalgeographic.com/animals/pufferfish/#pufferfish-closeup.jpg

This website has information and many fun facts about puffer fish.

Ocean Today: Weird Animals: Blackspotted Puffer Fish

http://oceantoday.noaa.gov/weirdanimals_blackspottedpufferfish

This website from the National Oceanic and Atmospheric Administration shows the blackspotted puffer swimming and talks about where it lives.

INDEX

Page numbers in **boldface** are illustrations. Entries in **boldface** are glossary terms.

ABOUT THE AUTHOR

From amazing animals to jellybeans, **Alicia Klepeis** loves to research fun and out-of-the-ordinary topics that make nonfiction exciting for readers. Alicia began her career at the National Geographic Society. She is the author of numerous children's books, including *Bizarre Things We've Called Medicine, Brain Eaters: Creatures With Zombielike Diets*, and *The World's Strangest Foods*. She has seen puffer fish at the Sydney Aquarium in Australia. Alicia lives with her family in upstate New York.